WHAT IS THE PURPOSE OF YOUR VISIT?

For Frankie:
It's been wonderful knowing
you.
   With best wishes,
      Wanda

Also by Wanda Barford

Sweet Wine and Bitter Herbs
A Moon at the Door
Losing, Finding

for David

Biting my truant pen, beating myself for spite,
'Fool,' said my Muse to me; 'look in thy heart and write.'
Sir Philip Sidney, *Astrophel and Stella*

WHAT IS THE PURPOSE OF YOUR VISIT?

Wanda Barford

IN ASSOCIATION WITH THE EUROPEAN JEWISH PUBLICATION SOCIETY

Acknowledgements

Some of these poems have appeared in the following magazines:
Acumen, *'14' Magazine*, *The Jewish Quarterly*, *The Morley Review*,
Other Poetry, *Resurgence*; and the following anthologies:
In the Company of Poets, edited by John Rety (Hearing Eye),
Messages, edited by Naomi Lewis (Faber and Faber).

First published in Great Britain in 2006 by Flambard Press
Stable Cottage, East Fourstones, Hexham NE47 5DX
www.flambardpress.co.uk

In association with the European Jewish Publication Society
PO Box 19948, London N3 3ZJ
www.ejps.org.uk

The European Jewish Publication Society gives grants
to support the publication of books relevant to Jewish
literature, history, religion, philosophy, politics and culture.

Typeset by BookType
Cover design by Gainford Design Associates
Printed in Great Britain by Cromwell Press, Trowbridge, Wiltshire

A CIP catalogue record for this book
is available from the British Library.
ISBN 1 873226 79 9

Flambard Press wishes to thank Arts Council England
for its financial support.

Flambard Press is a member of Inpress
and of Independent Northern Publishers.

Contents

What Is the Purpose of Your Visit?

What is the purpose of your visit?
Those who sent me did not disclose it.

Do you mean to stay long?
It's not up to me to determine the length of my stay.

Will you be usefully employed?
(*sotto voce* – I wonder what do you mean by 'useful')
Employment is almost always useful.

Will you be a burden on the state?
I hope not to be a burden on anyone, least of all myself.

Have you got somewhere you can live?
I can live anywhere, where I can see the sky.

Do you have a permanent address?
Yes, for the moment, in the Street of Life.

Do you speak our language fluently?
No, but I like all language, and I promise
to apply myself diligently to yours.

SO GOODBYE TWENTIETH CENTURY

This strange century
With its slaughter of the innocent
Its flight to the moon –

Charles Simic, 'Street Scene'

And What Were You Doing on D-Day?

It's the day of my music exam – Theory Grade 5.
In assembly there's a service for the boys who will get killed.
Either side of me the girls are crying,
but I'm rehearsing my triads: major, minor, inverted . . .

At regular intervals ('Identify these intervals as:
augmented, diminished, concordant or dissonant')
news bulletins are read out in sombre tones
('Describe semitones and quarter-tones').

OUR BOYS ARE MAKING RAPID ADVANCES
BUT THE GERMANS ARE COUNTERING THIS OPENING PHASE
WITH SOME VICIOUS FIGHTING. ('Write an answering phrase
to balance the given phrase.')

On the wireless
a colonel hums a cheery tune;
his men sing in chorus but flattish . . .
('What is the function of flats, sharps, and naturals?')

IN THE LAST TWO DAYS
OUR BOYS HAVEN'T SLEPT MUCH.
('Insert rests where necessary
to complete these bars.')

('Give the Italian for: hurrying,
in the style of a march; with fire;
repeat from the beginning.') *Affrettando,*
alla marcia, con fuoco, da capo.

('What is the English equivalent of:
schnell, bestimmt, kräftig?')
THE GERMANS ARE REPLYING TO OUR ATTACKS
SWIFTLY, DECISIVELY, WITH ENERGY.

('Write a rhythm on one note
to fit the given words:
"Still do the stars impart their light
To those who travel in the night".')

My rhythm is for side-drum and bugles;
it's a funeral march in common time.
I'd like it to have a tune
and to be played *morendo*.

Now the Twentieth Century's Gone

'O dark, dark, dark, amid the blaze of noon.'
Milton, *Samson Agonistes*

It's the faces I'll be missing most; my mother's
fleshy half-moon cheeks, and father's greying temples.
And my brother impersonating Hitler,
with tightened lips and sporting a black moustache,
his hair sleek and Brylcreemed
for the 'war appeal' show that 'brought the house down'.

And the hazy, unburied faces
of those cut off before I knew them well . . .
cousins' child-faces, those of five-year-old twins,
brown eyes injected with burning liquid by Mengele's
nurses determining the genetic cause for the colour
of twins' eyes, if they differed from their mother's.

I'll even miss the fear – it haunted my childhood
(haunts me still): the standing on railway platforms
clutching at luggage, heading into the unknown –
like explorers of old setting off into the hinterland,
forced to carve out their own path, mapless –
our compass the absolute need to go.

We were the pioneers in the Republic of the Refugee.
At the *Café de la Paix* in the sick heart of Europe,
we sat at small round tables sipping bitter coffee,
learning of quotas. Some just back from an embassy
suggested Argentina; others Uruguay – 'lovely city Montevideo';
yet others the British colonies where money mattered.

Some sat sullen, wondering if
they'd survive being deracinated,
knowing too that roots
can be more fragile than plants
(so many since have been trekking over the planet
without luggage, with torn clothes and bleeding feet).

And now I see those other faces, emaciated and crumbling,
peering out of slits meant for cattle;
hollow-eyed faces that can no longer smile.
Almond-eyed Armenian faces; barbed-wire-torn faces;
trench faces; Killing-Fields-skull faces; Belsen faces;
the faces-I'm-too-ashamed-to-face faces.

But I look up into the sky and see
smoke-ring faces rising from the chimneys.
Now they're far from earth, far from danger,
they round themselves into fleshy rosy faces
that smile with their lips and their eyes,
and smile and disappear.

Family History

My uncle played the mandolin
at sunset under the window
of that girl from Kos.

Her skin was translucent;
her hair lit by the sinking sun,
shone like gold filaments.

Soon they married,
went to live in Milan
but he died young.

Twice he'd tracked over the Alps
to find safety for his family
in a refugee camp that claimed to be full.

She became a recluse,
her pale face suspended
like a lantern over her black dress.

For my wedding gift
she gave me silver coffee-spoons
in a neat leather case.

I've kept them there,
each one wrapped in tissue-paper
like a shroud; I haven't used them.

The Violin

Today the fiddle's out of tune –
a *scordatura* of twisted gut-strings
and shrieking horsetail hair.

Yesterday notes from Bach's Chaconne
rose, strong and pure, out of the hut
into the stinking air.

Before being marched off
the prisoner hid his violin
under his bunk, in the guard's stare.

*

And now I hear that violin –
a bird resurrected on the airwaves . . .
It's Holocaust Memorial Day.

Betrayal

I thought I saw her
in a street in Rome
wearing her bombazine dress
with white collar and cuffs –
she seemed unsteady
as she shuffled along in her soft slippers.

Her greying hair
was pulled back in a bun
as it had been
when her strong hands
lifted me up by the armpits,
singing: '*mia bella bambina*'.

I lurched forward
crying: '*Giovanna, Giovanna* . . .'
but my voice died
down the long street.
How could she have heard
from a lifetime away?

I wanted so much to tell her
how sorry I'd been to leave her,
to leave Milan,
the flat, my room, my toys –
that I'd been a bad girl
and would she please forgive me.

Letter from Beatrice

Not content, *caro* Alighieri, with following me round
the streets of Florence, when I was barely nine,
you come and disturb me here in Purgatory.

What a good thing I died young – just twenty-four –
while you pursued your amours relentlessly.
So what are you doing in this place among the dead?

One live man surrounded by so many shades
is enough to make us all shiver, make us feel old.
Why do you come to us here, when back on earth

you followed others of uncertain virtue?
Listen to the golden angels singing
and covering me in a rain of flowers.

Go back among the living. Remember Eurydice?
She'd forgotten what Orpheus looked like.
I'm just the same – I want peace and oblivion.

From Up There

i.m. D.J. Enright (1920–2002)

'I heard such bangings and such drillings –
what are you doing to our house?'

Just a little decorating, dear,
but not enough to scare a mouse.

'You always were a restless creature,
who could not just leave well alone.

You should practise quiet and stillness;
how to rest a stiffened bone.'

But down here I'm quite excited
at the thought of fresh new paint

to cover up life's little smudges;
better work than 'sing a plaint'.

'Oh well, have it your own way, dear,
there's no brush, nor paint, nor pen, up here.'

Washing Machine

'There are things,' you said,
'I've been dying to wash for years.'
And you piled them in: trousers,
vests and pants, shirts, socks,
without sorting whites from coloureds.
Even blankets and bedspreads, though
I tried to explain wool fibres need
different treatment from cotton ones.

And then you went for my ethnic poncho,
the one I bought in the mountains above Málaga
when I went to Lorca's house in Fuente Vaqueros;
it came out half its size, the leafy pattern spoilt.
'I'll throw you in next,' you said.
I took it seriously, and fled.

Trust

for Sammy

A child came to me
to be looked after –
a five-year-old boy
('six in twenty-one days').

I treated him
to a gooey cake
which he finally found too sweet,
and a three-sugar-lump hot chocolate.

We did sums
where magically plusses and minuses
were interchangeable; and we laughed
at waxwork-figures with unmatching heads.

And then it was bedtime
with cuddles from Panda and Golly
and a big hug from me;
and prayers in a strange language

which, like the idea of 'oneness',
or that the Lord will care for you,
must be taken on trust . . .

For Life

with thanks to Billy Collins

'All I need is a pen' –
my broad-nibbed Parker,
with black rather than blue ink
(black has a kind of permanence)
and sheets of A4, unlined.

I would need my desk
its pigeon-holes stuffed with old diaries;
and the flap that shuts when not in use.
The chair should be modest
but well-adjusted to my spine.

I also need light, lots of it.
If not flooding in naturally,
my standard lamp with 150-watt bulb
is a must to assist my failing eyes,
and discourage gloomier imaginings.

And I would need my heart
with its accumulated baggage
of yeses and nos and maybes,
forever on the edge of something radiant
to take me to the stars and back.

How It Really Was

When Rudolf Nureyev died in 1993
they showed him laid out
in a rosewood box, silk-lined,
with brass corners and superior nails.

People filed past
to kiss his face
but he wasn't really there.

No; you see he'd been dancing a pas-de-deux
in the Blue Bird and the Princess Florine,
his body covered in sapphire and silver feathers
and his hands ceaselessly fluttering, when
at the final brisé, he took a huge leap upwards
and away he went through the painted sky.

The audience waited
for him to reappear . . .

Trees Chatter Amongst Themselves

'You're pretty useless,' the orange-tree said to the cypress,
'you don't produce anything. Now look at my oranges,
beautifully round and golden – they quench people's thirst
and top up their vitamin C level.'

And the olive-tree next door piped up: 'My fruit
may be small and unassuming, often wrinkled,
but it's very tasty and produces tons of oil
which (they've discovered at last) is good for the heart.'

Then together they chant: 'You're ever so refined,
you get taller and slimmer each year. That way
you think you get closer to God;
but that's just being snooty and arrogant.'

The cypress replied quietly, in measured tones:
'The purpose of things is not immediately apparent.
I do have one – my wood serves to make coffins.
I don't mind giving up my life for someone's comfort in death.

The Bard honoured me once with a song':
and in a mellow baritone it sang,
   'Come away, come away Death,
   And in sad cypress let me be laid.

I am the tree that graces those shadowy Umbrian hills;
I'm on the Tuscan slopes behind Mary's head;
I echo the Christ child's finger pointing to heaven;
I am the link between the earth and the sky.

I'm an aspiration, a longing . . .
men do not live by olives and oranges alone.'

. . . and the wind rustled all their leaves.

From the Bed Opposite

Royal Free Hospital, Hampstead, 2001

Can you help me?
Is there a drink . . .
can someone help me?
Something to drink . . . to drink.

I want to sit up
can someone help me?
Nurse, nurse,
make me sit up.

Someone hold my hand.
Please, where's Richard.
Are you Jewish?
Can you call Richard.

Someone get me out . . .
I can't breathe,
open the window, nurse,
why isn't the window open?

I want my son,
why isn't he here?
I want to go home,
why can't I go home?

No, take that away,
I just want water.
My mouth's dry,
give me some water.

Just leave me . . .
I'm uncomfortable,
nurse, I want to . . .
can you take me to the loo?

I don't need that thing,
I don't want anything.
I'm not able, not able . . .
take those things away.

What is this place . . .
where am I?
How will I pay for this?
Where's my son? Call my son.

Please don't put those bars up,
I won't fall out.
Put those bars down
they hurt my knees.

Make me sleep
put me so I can sleep.
In the morning you will
call my son, won't you?

In Borgo San Sepolcro

I asked three old men
where I could find Piero.
'Che Piero vuole?' shouts one.
'Quello della Francesca,' his friend nudges him.
'Vada di là, quella strada lì.'

Five hundred years melt . . .
I'm on my way to Francesca's;
I see the widow lift washing to the line,
her son pore over his geometry books.
But they'd pointed down a narrow street
to the Municipal Gallery.

It was a still day,
the *pinacoteca* empty of people.
From its cracked walls 'Death
thou shalt die' came at me,
and the so-vertical, marmoreal
figure of Christ, one foot
on the lip of the sarcophagus,
ready to step up, to walk the world,
his straight banner flying.

Sprawled on the ground
the four soldiers, drunk with sleep,
one with both hands over his eyes,
have heard nothing, suspect nothing.
When they wake, they'll have to be told,
to be sat down and told
what had happened.

The Balcony Room

Painting by Adolph Menzel (1815–1905), Nationalgalerie, Berlin

In the first freshness of the day
You've gone outside – you're on the balcony,
Perhaps. But your chair, empty now, stands firmly
In the breeze that swells the white organza drapes.

The other chair's reflected
In the long mirror which tells
Of inscape and of escape, of where
Illusion lies. But we must trust
The light and lightness of the room,
Its eloquent restraint – how it cannot yield
To us the secret of unfinished things:
The end of the rug we cannot see,
The picture's golden frame the mirror hides,
Nor the room's most distant, furthest sides.

Domgasse Fünf

*'My compliments to dear Theresa, the maid who waits
on me here is also a Theresa – but Heavens! How
different from our Theresa from Linz, in beauty,
virtue, charms – and a thousand other merits!'*
    Mozart in a letter to his father of 1780

Liebe Mutti:
Last night – well, one o'clock – the master died,
and though I wasn't fond of him, I cried.
His 'Stanzi' really went berserk, forgot
to feed her son, just left him in his cot,
and sent me rushing down the stony steps
to fetch them water from those slithery taps;
I tripped and gashed my knee, but no-one cared.
Last week a black-cloaked man arrived who stared
and chilled me through. 'Where's the Requiem,' he said,
'it should be done by now, unless he's dead.'
And as I showed him out and shut the door
I heard such banging from the upper floor
as made my heart leap out. He wanted air,
the windows opened wide: 'It isn't fair
to feel so weak and have these fainting fits . . .'
He'd ask Süssmayr to write the missing bits.

Today the doctor came and then the priest.
What cheek to think I'd poisoned him, at least
that's how it seemed from all their questioning.
Then dear St Stephen's bells began to ring . . .
I thought I heard the master rise and sing
with friends and pupils as he'd done before.
But now I'm tired, I shan't write any more.

I'll try a new house when the funeral's done
A far less noisy place, but with some fun.
Expect me back in Linz next Thursday night.
Here comes my lady and she looks a fright.

Your loving daughter

Theresa

this fifth day of December 1791

Bridge

I stood on the bridge
Facing the river.
Neither the bank I had left
Nor the one I was going to
Seemed important, but
The bridge held me;
Held my body firm
And my mind focussed.

I stand on the bridge
Facing the river.
Neither the bank I have left
Nor the one I am going to
Seem important, but
The bridge holds me
And I loosen to the flow
Of the water below.

I shall stand on the bridge
Facing the river.
Neither the bank I shall have left
Nor the one I shall be going to
Will seem important, but
The bridge will hold me
And I shall be drawn
By the water below.

Veins

I hadn't foreseen how spidery
your veins would become, and greeny-brown
like the tracery on these dry leaves.

That other autumn when you took me to Carrara
we both admired the miniature crucifix
where the marble's veins coincide

with those in Christ's legs and arms:
'è stato fatto da Michelangelo',
they told us in the village.

Pool

I'm no Alice,
I don't have her curiosity, her stamina;
yet, as I stood at the sink the other night,
I noticed my feet
were in three inches of water.

I looked beyond,
into the dining-room, the hall, the studio –
water was seeping through the carpet
everywhere;
it began to swirl and the house to heave
like a ship afloat.

I didn't taste the water for salt,
I knew it was mainly tears
accumulated under the floorboards
over the years.
Still, I felt confident . . .

Alice, I remembered,
hadn't drowned but floated.

The Guest

Yes, there was someone uninvited
at the wedding feast – someone
the bride had known since childhood.
He belonged to the past, she told herself.

One wide sunset, close to the trunk
of a great tree, when she and the tree
and the sunset were one, he'd been there,
barefoot on the grass . . .

or that other time on a southbound ship,
when she'd stood on the deck watching the moonlit wake
and listening to the water churning,
there he was, his head among the stars.

But here at the wedding?
What was he doing sitting upright
at one end of the high table,
his formal black suit against the crisp white cloth.

Next morning he was there again,
in the large gilt mirror of the hotel bedroom;
and in the dining-room at supper at a nearby table,
laughing and oblivious of her this time.

How often through her life
would he go on turning up,
in what unlikely places? Surely at her funeral
he'd be no mere spectator.

La Serenissima

I

Like Venice
I have built
canals inside me
to wash my bedrock
with gentle, lapping water.

Boats that pass by
crowded with unknowns,
others propelled
by a lonely man with an oar,
only ruffle the surface.

Tall dark houses
with mossy landing-stages
line the canals inside me;
behind high arched windows
dramas are enacted.

And I have known
subterranean canals
that never see the sun
and pass under
the tall dark houses,

under the fondamenta,
the shadowy calles,
the twisty ramos;
under the sotoportegos
and the campi . . .

and quite without warning
flow out into the lagoon,
out to open sea
where the end
and the beginning merge.

II

How will it be in old age?
Will the canals be darker behind the houses?
The landing stages more slippery?
The gondoliers be singing out of tune?

When first I saw her I was four years old
And chasing pigeons round St Mark's Square;
Father held a brace of them on his arm,
And mother posed in tilted hat and spotty dress.

Then we sailed the Adriatic
In a white, white ship
With the captain handsome all in white
And the band playing '*Ma tu pallida luna perchè*'.

III

Now I've seen her in old age;
The canals inside me are still there
But they're brighter, their lapping more musical;
Their ever-changing surface more silvery.

Dramas behind high-arched windows
Are stilled, transmuted into Goldoni-like
Commedias with elaborate costumes
That disguise youth's raw emotions.

Their eyes are often masked – do they smile or weep? –
And their faces whitened, covering all blemishes;
Abundant gowns hide abundant curves.
I no longer fear the mask might fall.

One Country

The land of the living
and the land of the dead
are all one country
when dreaming.

And the ones who for years
have not lifted their heads
are with us again
in our dreaming.

And the ones who are living
will wither and die
without warning or sign
in the dreaming.

And even at times
(and you never ask why)
one long since dead will die
in the dreaming.

There's a field open wide
with no barbed-wire or fence,
no soldier on guard
in the dreaming.

And all seem alive
with no hint of pretence
in the borderless land
of our dreaming.

Fox

Ginger fox, wild visitor to my tidy garden,
bring me lightning thoughts that swish back and forth
like your tail. Give me eyes that pierce through surfaces;
a nose that picks up the scent
of what is good and what rotten.

Fearless fox, let me live like you
down where the dark is natural and holds no dread.
Teach me to bristle only at real peril,
not at small, insignificant dangers
that churn up the stomach each day.

Wild fox, come back to my tidy garden.

Your Eyes

for Miriam who made tapestries

Your eyes were needle-sharp
when first I met you – they were
the warp and weft of all your life.
They probed and explored,
linking a mere point to infinity.

They shone their beam
right over me, like the silken
gold-and-silver thread
that heightens a line
on your tapestries.

And those eyes saw into me,
set me to find the still centre
of my turning world; to remember
the sea-substance of which we're made
and the star-dust too.

Your hair was golden then –
a halo your laughter
soon dispelled; no angel you.
Your feet are in earthly things,
your head is in the stars.

Africa's child, you understood
the black man's closeness to his land –
that red earth we seldom see in Europe.
In your works we touch the mud
and thatch of their huts,

the clay of their pots,
their shiny-skinned, round-bellied
babies; the mother's head balancing
the water jug, her arms
pounding mealie flour.

In England's more subtle climate
you wove the all-seeing eye
into inner vision, the sea
into one huge multi-coloured wave,
the wind's gust became breath.

Then you tapestried Oakwood Court
your mansion block, depicting architecture
in multi-layered woollen threads.
How lively it became, all that red brick –
almost African!

And in middle age you turned
to your roots in the Bible: the bush
burning with no person there – only footprints
displacing the sand – an absence to be filled
again and again and again.

Now you're frail. Your body
suppled once by dancing and tai chi
moves stiffly into the rigid frame.
But your eyes, still bright,
light up the space between us.

Schoolroom in Baghdad

This seven-year-old at her desk
with dark eyes and brown hair,
in a crisp white blouse
(despite the shortage of water)
could easily be me, but long before
the picture of *Il Duce* and *Vittorio Emmanuele Terzo*
had been removed from the textbooks.

We sang '*Giovinezza*' every day,
proud to be part of this youth;
while my brother, dressed as a *Balilla*,
stepped out in his shiny black boots,
and father from the window
of our seventh-floor flat shouted
'*Viva Mussolini*' when the motorcade went by.

So why one day,
when we were so eager to participate,
was I sent home from school . . .
Homework not done? Inattentive in class?
Dirty behind the ears? Then again sent home
from a different school, to no school at all,
to losing those friends I'd made.

Now in Baghdad Saddam Hussein no longer smiles
from the title-page of books, from posters or portraits.
How long will the children remember him? As I
remember Mussolini: his jutting chin,
his roaring speeches from the balcony of Palazzo Venezia –
'*meglio un giorno da leone, che cent'anni da pecora*' –
his farcical imitation of a Roman emperor.

Baghdad means 'Abode of Peace'.
My city was Milan slipping ever closer to war.
Hers is the city of 'The Thousand and One Nights'.
Mine was the cradle of the Sforzas, dukes of Milan
in the dark and bloodied Castello we'd visit
for Sunday outings. Now Baghdad is bloodied too –
snipers in the streets; guards escort the children to school.

Commemoration at the Holy City of Karbala

*This is a Shia pilgrimage centre where Husain, martyr
and grandson of Mohammed, was murdered in 680.*

This baby boy
with two milk teeth
peeping out of his lower gum,
his face creased with sobs,
terror distorting his dark eyes
as he senses his mother's grief,
while she slaps her face in anger
over and over – knows nothing
of modes of worship,
whether Sunni or Shia,
but may grow up
with a painful memory
of this holy fountain
sprouting blood-red water,
or sometimes, like today,
disgorging blood.

Journeying on Without You

Like a ship leaving harbour
To the melancholy sound of the horn,
Relinquishing familiar things – the coastline,
Summer beaches with fine sand where toddlers
Learn to walk; and the escort of seagulls
Turning back for scraps nearer land –
Like a ship whose prow is set
To cut through colder unknown seas . . .

So too I journey away from you;
Further with each passing year,
Further from those last moments together
When I stroked your hair and felt your skull,
And thought (not spoke) of this strange journey
Away from you and then, at last, towards you.

Finis

'All the world's a stage,
And all the men and women merely players.'
Shakespeare, *As You Like It*

Strike the set:
Store the props
Pull down the backcloth
Fold up the wings
Fly out the tabs
Rip up the marks
Roll up the carpets
Lift the floor
Un-focus the lights
De-rig them and
Close the barn doors.
Release the prompt.

Unmask the actors
Dis-mantle them and
Discard their costumes.
Shelve the script
Draw the curtains
Drop the iron.

Can you still hear distant clapping?

SINGING LIKE A WOMAN IN LOVE

A Sonnet Sequence Celebrating Love in Old Age

'Cantando come donna innamorata'

Dante Alighieri, *Purgatorio*, Canto XXIX

You Left Paris First

And now you've gone –
And half of me's gone too.
We stood on bridges looking at the Seine:
Its barges, *bâteaux-mouches*, their V-shaped wakes,
And wondered how it could be
We were so in love
At an age as ridiculous as ours –
The curving spine, the sagging skin . . .

Yet love there was,
As vigorous and strange
As any younger love might be,
And maybe twice as loyal
For all the knowledge of deep hurt,
For all the life already lived.

5 a.m.

I stretched out my hand
To touch if you were there
In real flesh – that I hadn't
Imagined your body-warmth,
The feel of your moulded thighs,
That quick response of tiny kisses
Along my outward-curving back
Smoothly fitting into you.

And yes, you clasped my hand,
Held it like a traveller reaching land
After a voyage longer than it should have been . . .
And yes our bodies said, yes, these trees,
These skies, these singing leaves
Are ours, the new world of our discovery.

Waking Separately

In the grey morning
I didn't wait for you to wake.
Your body was too heavy on the bed;
Your head sunk deep into the pillows.

As for me, I drank in the light,
Opened up the grey sky
To read in it; to clear the mist
To understand; to see.

And then you woke bewildered,
Why was I not there beside you,
Where had I gone and why?
(But a part of me was there.)

And then the sun brought us together –
The climbing sun with its promise of heat.

Voices

We each hold on to voices from the past
That lived and rang in bodies long since dead.
Set free, even those voices cannot last
Though still they often echo in the head.
It's we who summon them to make them live
And let them share the banquet of our joy,
And sit, true spirits at the feast, and give
Some living light to what we might destroy.

For look, dear love, how we're alive – no worms
Eat up our flesh as yet, nor strip a bone –
We live and sing and throb in earthly forms;
And there's no sin for which we need atone.
We'll join those voices soon enough, when we,
As sure as sun will rise, shall cease to be.

No Photo Yet

We haven't got a snapshot of us two,
Not yet – and if we did how could it catch
Those many things the camera fails to show:
The tingling nerves, dry mouth and racing pulse.

Diverting smiles would hide a deeper seam –
An inkling of beauty's Rilkean terror
We'd hardly just begun to understand . . .
And holding hands, as we might wish to do,

Could not stave off the sense of separateness
That haunts the flesh; nor distance us one speck
From the mysterious world where souls, they say,
Are snatched away by that remorseless click.

But here we go, we've tried but can't avoid
Being immortalized on celluloid.

We Take a Walk in the Vale of Health

We stopped to hear the wind fluster the leaves
Of ancient willows swishing by the pond;
But overhead a plane destroyed the song
Of reedy oboes in the woodwind breeze.

And I, transported back some fifty years
To where I lodged at 'Ashdown' on the edge
Of adulthood – a student ripe for knowledge
But racked by crippling, insubstantial fears.

I can recall my frozen attic room
Where children set a mousetrap near my bed;
The shrieking mouse was caught, but not its head . . .
It's shrieking still, inside the memory's gloom.

Then, by the Byron house we left the Vale,
Back in the now of you, the past grows pale.

You

A smooth high forehead like a plover's egg;
Your peasant's hands, rough-skinned and always cold;
One normal and one swollen stockinged leg;
Your Oxford voice too self-assured, too bold.

My front-door mat too small for your big feet;
Two hairs protruding from your pimpled nose;
Your belly proof of how you over-eat.
Bifocals add a professorial pose.

But then I love your laughter and your face;
Your intellectual honesty of mind.
I love your gestures and the natural grace
With which you deal with others, always kind.

But most the way you gag me with a kiss;
Not to see you for a day – the abyss.

Nightmare

Your wife's come back –
She'd been pretending to be dead,
Just to give you a break, she said,
A rest from nursing her.
You race home – try to phone me
But you've forgotten my number,
And you're losing the outline of my face.
The colour of my voice.

Six months or so along,
You suddenly remember me –
Look me up in the phone book.
You say: 'I haven't forgotten you,
But my place is here; this is where I belong
Send me a poem sometime . . .'

The Years

'What is it to grow old?
Is it to lose the glory of the form,
The lustre of the eye?'
    Matthew Arnold, 'Growing Old'

If I were younger say, by thirty years,
I'd like to pleasure you with such delights
As Cleopatra showered on Antony
When he lay powerless in her swarthy arms;
Or Héloïse revealed to Abelard
The scholar steeped in books, but green in love;
Or youthful Juliet offered Romeo
Her lord, her love, her friend, all three in one.

But I am old. My body's scarred and bruised.
My skin is pale – my make-up's thicker now.
My neck is sinewy; my hands are veined.
I do not sleep so well; my vision's blurred.
Yet, if despite all this you love me still,
My cooling blood will stir again, it will . . .

Shouting It

'L'amor che move il sole e l'altre stelle.'
   Dante Alighieri, *Paradiso*

Are you listening, trees and leaves,
Are you listening, skies,
Clouds, winds and seas?
Are you listening, oceans,
Islands, coral reefs and cliffs,
Suns, moons, most distant stars,
Circling planets, energetic quasars?
Do listen to this rhythm, much like yours . . .

It's no vague whisper or a lover's sigh,
More like a mother's love, a lullaby;
A rocking movement coursing through all things
That keeps the stars in their appointed place;
Eternal balance music does so well –
The name is love, the absence of it, hell.

At Montparnasse Cemetery

You put a pebble on my mother's grave;
You hadn't known her, but knew her enough
Through me – how she'd been sensitive but tough,
Uncompromising with herself and brave.

And holding up my book you read aloud
The list of neighbours there: Baudelaire, Zadkine,
Beckett, the dulcet-voiced Sablon, Soutine . . .
Their closeness would, for sure, have made her proud.

And then incised into a wide headstone
We saw both Star and Cross lie side by side.
Alive, as here in death, they'd not denied
Their roots, commingled then, as here their bones.

And you, *ma belle*, beneath your marble stele,
Teach me to live, with all your former zeal.

Bridges

'Les mains dans les mains restons face à face
        Tandis que sous
    Le pont de nos bras passe
Des éternels regards l'onde si lasse.'
        Apollinaire, 'Le Pont Mirabeau'

We ride across Westminster Bridge again,
My cheek against the collar of my coat,
Yours brushing up the other side of it . . .
Are you remembering bridges on the Seine?

But this is London, more austere, more straight;
Big Ben looks down to see that we behave . . .
I sometimes sense you rue the past and crave
Times on the Terrace sipping tea till late.

Yet the Wheel shows us Time is slow to move;
We have a chance to fill this little space
With reckless kisses, or a quick embrace.
Let's do it, make a monument to love.

And look, each pod is giving us a wink,
As if to say, yes, live life to the brink

And Still We're Two

Your modulated voice calls down the phone
But without lips or tongue or spicy taste,
With these vibrations of your voice alone
I feel monastic, void of fun, too chaste.

Tonight you're here, your body twined with mine;
And still we're two ('Oh Wherefore?' Shelley cried).
We never can obliterate that line
That separates two souls, though many tried.

In stone at times the two are fused in one –
See ancient kists, or mother-child at birth –
But in reality it can't be done;
We carry it as an ideal on earth.

Yet separateness is pleasing to old age,
We must have space enough to vent our rage.

A Darker Place

To be without you
Is to be diminished –
A tortoise withdrawn into its shell.
You set me in the sunlight,
Give me warmth; my carapace sparkles.
I touch the sand, the stones,
The earth, and feel connected –
A tiny part of an infinite pattern.

Strange then how frequently
I need my shell –
Need to escape into a darker,
Quieter, more solitary place,
Where to be alive is to be alone,
To be alone and think of you.

SHADOWS AND MOUNTAINS

A Sequence of Poems

(Study Tour of Israel 2000
with the Council of Christians and Jews)

'How beautiful upon the mountains are the feet
of him that bringeth good tidings.'

Isaiah, Chapter 52, Verse 7

Phoenix

'When the Lord overturned the captivity of Zion,
we were like them that dream.'
    Psalm 126

The El Al Boeing 747
with blue bands on its white body
has a Star of David on its upright tail.

When I looked out of the window,
we were flying, the pilot told us
in Hebrew, over Germany.

Encounter

I met Abraham today
walking over a dune with his goats and his camels,
and I greeted him warmly
in my best Biblical voice.

And he, not at all patriarchal,
said: 'When I left my Sarah
at dawn this morning, she was still laughing.
You see, we'd had three very odd visitors
who insisted she'd soon be pregnant. But at her age?
Besides I already have a son.

And I do miss Lot my nephew
who settled in the lush country around Sodom.
Forgive me, I should be enquiring after *your* family.'

But as I was about to tell him
how my grandparents went up in smoke
he vanished . . . only the tinkly sound
of goat bells hung on the Negev air,
now louder, now softer,
over the undulating sands.

At Ra'hel's Tomb

I saw a lizard scuttle over your headstone
as if he knew your lines: 'tiny joys,
joys like a lizard's tail'. And I held
the rusty chain your book's attached to
in my hand, but let go your words
with their 'hints and mysteries' into the air,
into the sky above this blue, blue Kinneret.
And someone read aloud your poem 'Perhaps'
that struggles to fend off
the 'cold wind of certainty'.
Yet certain it was you had to abandon
the work you loved: night-milking
under 'the terror of the moon',
but soothed by 'the cow's warm breathing'.
And at forty-one you were dead
and they brought you here
to your 'Garden of Perhaps'
which is not a cemetery
but a place where 'the dead don't die'.

Stones

i.m. Jehuda Amichai

Pink stones of Jerusalem at sunrise.

Violet stones of Jerusalem at sunset.

Put your ear to the stones in the wall,
you'll hear them wailing; and they're damp
with the breath of prayers. Sometimes
they whisper their fear to the cracks
where rolls of paper crush the grasses.

Proud stone
that bore the head of Jacob
as he dreamt of angels on a ladder
linking earth to heaven.

Stones ready in buckets,
in bags at street corners in Hebron.

David with just one stone,
a smooth stone (one of five from the river),
slew the giant Philistine of Gath . . .
but this is no Goliath –
it's a small boy
cowering behind his father.

Look, all these stones have been turned,
but there's nothing underneath them.

Listen, this stone's deaf
from the yells that surround it.

See, this one's blinded
by the horror it's seen.

And this one's still and cold,
pretending to be dead, until
a small boy lifts it,
holds it in his hand,
aims and kills.

What are stones
in the language of the earth?
In Greek *petros* is stone,
which is Peter, which is church.
And Jerusalem has so many churches;
and blood has seeped into its ancient stones.

Blood-red stones of Jerusalem at noon.

Violet stones of Jerusalem at sunset.

Pink stones of Jerusalem at sunrise.

Tabgha (Place of Seven Springs)

Our pews are tree-stumps,
our choir's the wind,
the lapping waves its antiphon.

We look up to the sky,
our altar, and down
to the sand, our hassock.

Not through stained glass
does the sun filter its rays
but through slits in the raffia roof.

The celebrant recites a psalm
partly drowned
by the roar of the sea, our diapason.

And without fishes or loaves
we're fed and strengthened,
here by the shores of the Sea of Galilee.

Kibbutz Lavi

Girl from the Diaspora
who keeps her hands neat
for Mozart sonatas and their ornaments,
for the lilt of Chopin mazurkas –
their hands are rough and calloused,

but they know how to light candles
when the Sabbath slips in at sunset
like a timid bride
and everyone's dressed in white
to receive her.

Then the silence of the Sabbath day,
to be touched, felt, heard, savoured:
the percussion in the kitchen's stopped,
no one in the milking parlour, the laundry,
the winepress, all machinery unmanned.

And now voices rise
from the white-and-blue synagogue –
the boys beside their fathers
reading and rocking and chanting
and sitting and standing by turn.

Back at the kibbutz hotel, the girl
catches her reflection in the long mirror –
her matching London clothes,
her Louis Vuitton cases; the en-suite
bathroom, the cocktail cabinet –

and she feels doubly uneasy,
wondering why men and women are toiling
all day under the blistering sun, and at night
under arc-lights, to extend yet further
this four-star hotel.

Air-Conditioned Coach Through the Negev

'*Boker tov Amnon*,'
we greet our driver –
and he: '*Kacha, kacha* . . .'
and I admire his arched black eyebrows
in the rear-view mirror each day
as we settle on board.

Does he know he'd lusted after
his half-sister Tamar,
and pretended to be ill so
she'd come and nurse him?

But with us he's well and strong;
he's our water-carrier,
our path-finder,
frontline man at checkpoints.
He and the guide will protect us.

Tamar dutifully baked him some cakes
which he refused to eat
until they were alone together.
Then he raped her.

Amnon drives us to roadside cafés
where he eats with us and sips black coffee,
and tells us of his newest baby,
how he prefers to let his wife
get on with looking after it.

But soon Amnon tired of Tamar
and had his servant throw her out.
Two years later: 'Amnon beware,
beware your brother Absalom's
sheepshearing party . . .'

We have a farewell party
at the Olive Tree Hotel
but Amnon's not there,
he's at home with his wife;
we drink a 'thank you' to him.

FOUR SATIRES AND A PARODY

Mr Kalashnikov on TV

Good evening. Thank you.
You see small man, but have big mind;
I invent, invent. Last summer I make
gun – it works, how you say . . . a treat.

It is 0.5 calibre, with rapid-fire bore.
I give you details but you will be tired.
No, no I not politician, I not vote
in Yeltsin referendum – leave it.

In competition last year
my gun first prize, because light,
easy to use; boy can learn quickly,
to clean also. I so proud.

Boris sold many, many guns:
to Sierra Leone, Congo, Nigeria,
Somalia, Angola, Colombia.
But for me no money – I don't want.

I help Russia to get dollars.
She is my country – I love her.
In Chechnya too we use Kalashnikov,
also the rebels use. Goodnight.

PS 2003

And now I give my name to Vodka.
Do not drink Smirnoff, drink Kalashnikov;
is made from pure Russian grain, water filtered
from Lake Ládoga. You will feel fire!

Microwavable – or, The Suppression of Time

They've invented a microwave womb,
Commodious and warm, very snug,
Where the foetus can feel quite at home
And safe as a bug in a rug.

The baking procedure is quick –
Not nine months as always before,
But nine minutes flat, by the clock,
Then a rushing headfirst to the door.

Of course there's heartburn and backache
And sickness, but ever so slight,
With short bouts of nauseous dyspepsia,
And feeling the chest squeezed up tight.

But soon comes the moment of labour;
Yes, 'moment' for that is its length,
And mum can hardly be braver
Still giving it all of her strength.

Then she puts the wee one to her breast
Where it suckles for less than a tick
Latching on with vigour and zest.
But death comes equally quick.

Precautionary Verses for the Twenty-First Century

Breathe as little as you can, Nanny said,
For fear you might inhale unwelcome lead.

Even when you think you breathe fresh air
You're actually imbibing Legionnaire's.

And in water aluminium lurks
So avoid those public waterworks.

Mind you Vichy, Perrier and the local source
Could be spawning something far, far worse.

(I'll have a gin and tonic –
It staves off the old bubonic.)

And please, no egg, for salmonella
Jigs around your guts like Pulcinella.

Be sure you eat no beef, at least no brain,
If you'd rather NOT become insane.

You've heard of spongiform encephalopathy, bovine variety . . .
So better lead a life of great sobriety.

And pregnant mums avoid all cheeses
That may give your babe the wheezes.

For Brie and Camembert unpasteurized will breed Listeria
And encourage ugly phases of hysteria.

And as for white flour, butter, fat,
You really should have none of that.

Which leaves us with a friendly fag,
But I say NO; and don't mind if I nag.

Monsieur Nicot should have been hung
For all the damage to our lungs.

ENVOI

All this abstemiousness is such a strain . . .
We'll die of too much health, but with no pain.

Filling in Forms

'To which ethnic group do you belong?'

I'm Bangladeshi
born in Whitechapel, so
I'm a Cockney; I'll tick
'Asian British'.

I'm Pakistani
born in Rawalpindi, so
I can tick 'Asian, pure'.

I'm 'any other Asian background'.
I come from Mauritius, so
I'm Mauritian/Indian/Chinese.
But we were all British once,
and before that we were all French –
what does that make me now?

I'm Zambian
born in Brixton, so
I'm 'British-Black';
or is it 'Black-British'?

I'm Caribbean,
born in St Lucia of white parents
but mixed grandparents, so
I'm one quarter 'Black-Caribbean'.
(Will that do?)

I'm 'Any Other Black Background', but
I was adopted when I was one
by a white family in Glasgow
and they haven't told me
what my 'Black Background' is . . .

I'm Chinese and proud of it.
(We're older than you, you know.)
'Hong Kong Chinese? Taiwanese?
Or mainland China?' I shan't tell you.
Anyway we all have slitty eyes, don't we?

My father's a Yorkshireman
and mother's Turkish, so
I'm 'Mixed White and Asian'.
Sundays we have roast beef
with Bulgar-wheat pudding.

I have a Senegalese mother
and an Oxford father.
At home we're trilingual,
yes, 'Mixed Race', if you must . . .

My background's pretty mixed:
Spanish grandma, Jamaican granddad,
English father and Filipino mother.
What does that make me?
I'm getting confused . . .

Oh, what a relief!
I'm 'White, British'.
No problem – except of course
my ancestors were Huguenots.

O'Neill on one side,
O'Flannagan on the other;
what could we be but 'Irish'
and proud of it (forget those
awkward de Valeras who landed
with the Armada).

I'm a Jew –
grandfather was born in Riga.
Naturally I'm British, but . . .

not really 'Caucasian'; you see
I'm Semitic (as in anti-Semitic) so
do I tick 'White'?

I'm what *you* call 'Other',
and I want it to stay that way; so
I shan't tell you what 'Other'
stands for, not ever.

Onion

I love you, Onion,
Your rosy-hued delicious goldenness,
The tinkling piano-music of your crinkly skin.

Like the best of women
You hold your secret still!
Secretive Onion, with all your inwardness
Flowing inwardly, wombward,
Toward one orifice, one centre.

On your furry stool
You sit arrayed in gold
Like a fat Indian Goddess in her inwardness;
And I love remote secretness
That can be worshipped unrevealed.

The Italians vulgarly call you *cipolla*,
And they say it's female, of course.
But they slice your purple loveliness,
Your coyness, roughly with their knife,
With all their phallic intensity;
They cut you into pallid submission.
And you retaliate
From your ripe, juice-full womb
By making them spill
The bitter crocodile tears
Of loutish angry men.
Angry Italian men
Who cannot force their way quickly
Into your coiled and lovely places.

But I approach you
As I would a Mohammedan woman,
Unfolding her close-curtained darkness
Layer by layer, but with burning respect
For her inward, covert mystery.

Till, gently, you fall apart in my hands,
Exuding your opiate fumes.
And it's nearly the very end of you,
When you've given up that secret membrane,
That amniotic sac of you,
That innermost shred
Of your secret, incoiled being.

And I worship you then
As a Goddess, like the Egyptians did
In all their sageness and wisdom;
For they had wisdom, those ancient Egyptians:
The wisdom of the Earth that dances,
And the wisdom of Fire and Water,
And the wisdom of all Inner Darknesses –
Like yours – and they hung upon Isis
A golden necklace of shallots.

Taormina